# Mouthwords from my Brainhole

## Holly Hodgson

Presentation by *BookLeaf Publishing*

Web: www.bookleafpub.com

E-mail: info@bookleafpub.com

ISBN: 9789358318067

First edition 2023

# DEDICATION

To my son,


Before you I had absolutely no idea what my purpose was. Now I know. Being your mother is the greatest blessing and privilege. I savour every second we spend together knowing they are the happiest times of my life.


All my love now and always,


Mama

# ACKNOWLEDGEMENT

Thank you to these very important people:

My son Brody
My husband Ash
My parents Kim, Mike and my sisters Brittany and Libby
My grandparents; Marilyn and Dennis
My dear friends; Sebastian, Guy, Amy and Francesca.

Further acknowledgement:

The book's title "Mouthwords from my Brainhole" stems from a phrase shared by outstanding writer and comedienne Liz Feldman. It has always stuck with me as a funny representation of jumbled thoughts reaching a rather confused mouth.

Thank you Liz for many years of three Ls - L Word coverage, laughter and lesbianism.

# PREFACE

To all my friends who told me I "should share this but bet me that I never would" thank you. This has mostly been written out of spite.

# The Unspoken Plea

I remember where I was the moment I decided I
didn't want to live anymore.
I was engulfed in a towel far too big for my
body
With my hair dreading from weeks of
maltreatment sat on a bed shared
With a woman who never wanted to be there.
She'd told me differently at the start but the
spool soon started unravelling when What I had
And what I was
No longer served.

Air felt like daggers and every innate gulp filled
me with regret and a sense of
total failure
I never knew pain like this existed but how
befitting it should hurt so much to "be" I always
knew I'd come here
I'd come before, opened the door but never had
the will to walk through
This time was different the door has been thrown
off its hinges
I was watching my own end unfold and it was
thrilling

Before you knew that air I was choking on was
replaced with the click-clack of pills like
Tic-Tacs
Friction down my throat chased with vodka
I didn't want it to hurt
I just wanted to stop hurting

I laid myself down on the bathroom floor
counting over and over
Hoping when I got to a thousand I'd have gone
No more pain
No more disappointment
Just peace
The echo chamber of voices telling me this is for
the best silenced for once
And soon its just me
Its just me

I think of my mother who might never stop
crying
I think of my father who would blame himself
My sisters who would live a life without me and
all the memories I'd miss
Before they were made
I fail at even death

I called am ambulance and confessed my sins
I asked to be saved, for salvation, but only for
them

They ask "did you mean to end your life?"
I tell them, "yes but just this part"

# B

the indelible mark
the raging tempest
but here now
skin to skin
for all my life
you are the reason

# IV Play

5

Their fingers dance
a languid waltz,
Unveiling desires
Uncaging faults

# An Ode to Jennifer Beals

Jennifer Beals, hi
Its Holly
We don't know each other but
I wish we did
I loved you in "Flashdance"
"What a feeling!" holds a different meaning if
you are an overweight teen lesbian finding her
footing
Excuse the pun
Your footwork was great

Imagine my surprise when I rocket to older teen
To discover you in six series of lesbian drama
I devoured many a Monster Munch multipack
watching your character Bette
Move through significant moments in a power
suit
The love between Bette and Tina rewrote lesbian
herstory
If only it were real
I remain convinced it is
Should either of us ever divorce
You know where I am

# Rise and Fall

I wage war but only with myself
I give into the unyielding chase to find a better
rendition
Walls once white are mottled green
Painted with older versions of me
I smell the rot of lives shed to make way for
fresh flesh
Sickly sweet skin pushes through desperate to
meet the sun
We hold out hope she sticks around

# Woman's World

Strive for achievement but really crane your
neck
To rebuild you must first break
And bend and stretch
You must crack and twist and fracture
You must do more but make it appear as less,
speak more but not
Loudly, or interrupt or be too big or bold or
Take or give or give under condition but not
when someone watches
Unfavourable
Distasteful
You can lead but not stronger than he
Or in tandem with he
Be at the forefront but really back-end
Bite your tongue to save feelings
But bite it. Clean. Off.

# Nourishment

fall only to the feet of the people who feed you
when you are truly starving

# B II

i find the truest version of myself
reflected in your eyes
your tiny hand outstretched in mine
you are my very being
you are the stillness in the sky
when i feel i'm drowning in the chaos of sea
i will hold you until the end of my time
and pray that for the rest of yours
you love as loudly and deeply as you were loved
perfection exists only in you

# V

speak in ways that transcend words
and move to breathy pants
the rapid gasps and clutch on cloth
move waves across crushed velvet
immerse

# things I think about in the bath

When did time "begin?"
If rules exist to be followed then why are there exceptions?
How far do bald people go up when washing their face?
Why doesn't glue stick to the inside of the bottle?
In the word scent which letter is silent? S or C?
What ever happened to Noel from Hear'Say?

# Failure

I hope I never fail you
Though I repeatedly have failed myself
I have made untold mistakes
and left my fragmented mind untreated
I've traced steps instead of trod them
and crumpled that which should have been crisp
I've eaten through every emotion
I have tried to dig out what eats away
with blades so sharp they ricochet
Having you I live in a perpetual state of fear
that one day I will fail you
Not by act or omission I would never hurt you
but through one day crashing from the almighty
high
that remains so strong but feels so temporary
It is hard to sit with joy when she's always been
a visitor
never a permanent resident

# An ordinary day

Ordinary days are the best of days
Significance holds weight in utterance
There is no crescendo except those we make
ourselves
Cups of tea go cold often

We do not watch the clock
It is just superfluous
Time loses all semblance of meaning,
importance
When the mundane "mundanes"

The rapping of rain on window panes
Serves as a soundtrack to ordinariness
Book spines crack as the are bent
The day to day is exchanged for ferocity of
fantasy
That moves from page to page

The desire to wish these days away
For fanciful and more favourable
I cannot fathom a better speed to move at
Then one where you can breathe in

# Illuminate

You illuminate
I bathe in that light
My head is submerged but only my mouth fills
I catch every single word that falls out of yours
I let go to let God remind me of his existence
Because surely a being like you cannot be
attributed just to atoms
I have not known love before I knew your love
It feels redundant to only give you my heart
I would sooner give you every vein and organ
Each cell comprised to make me is locked in
feverish devotion for you
Through transformation and evolution all that
has changed is
I run out of things to offer but my promise to
grow with you
Roots grow out of my fingertips and between us
we hold a forest
and in that forest you are more than the moon
And you illuminate.

# Coming home

Slow steeping curve and winding of unrelenting
road
So close to stepping first into childhood home
Shoulders release, kicking boots off tired feet
Crisp pastry desserts presented, smiles
exchanged as intended
Years of homemade meals ensnare the senses
The cold surrenders at the door the warmth of
hugs long overdue
Legs are crossed in infant wonder
Conversation unravels from all to nothing but
total comfort remains
The safety of these walls and those held in them
Truly knows no bounds

# All the things you do not know

you do not know if you're truly loved
you only know what they tell you
you do not know if you are good
you only know what they tell you
you do not know if there is a god
you only know what they tell you
you do not know who the bad guy is
you only know what they tell you
you do not know if you should be here
you only know what they tell you
you do not know what waits in death
you only know what they tell you
you do not know if you are worth enough
you only know what they tell you
you must keep going to see what's next
even if its just to hear what they tell you

# Therapy

i prefer the filling feeling of food to people
the comfort brought by excess that weighs deep
in my chest
is far better than any therapy
of course the challenge arises when trying to
hold a conversation with a fig roll
therapy it is

# Dear Holly

Here we are, the games afoot but now we have a
copy of the rules to which we play
The manuscript is bound tightly
Only we can see the contents
I asked you to burn some pages but you wouldn't
listen to me
Don't break the habit of a lifetime now
I carved a space out for you
I was sure you'd come back
I knew you missed me
When it's just you and I we return to a place
where only we can find us
Where the gaps are caverns and slipping through
the cracks is a descent we can't come back from
You like it there sometimes it's a comfort it's a
truth
And it reads as familiar because alone no one
can question
Streams of consciousness and imagination that
feels so real merge into two
But when there's no medicine or doctors or
loved ones or friends it's just me you reflect back
to
And therein is our solace and danger and fear

But familiarity reigns supreme and you'd rather
spend a lifetime here some days than popping
pills and speaking on your heart
The mastery of malnourishing yourself is one
you and I have perfected
Feeding your body is an easy task
Feeding your mind is an infection
Isolation is when you're at your best or worst or
deeply affected
I don't ask you for permission I just ask you to
take a breather
Stop the blister packs and let the rickety racket
take over
Only for a minute I promise

Are you there?
I've lost you.

# Transformation

strength in removal
sum of them and none of them
grazing tips across sore ribs
up to the firing lines
no longer wincing but relishing
freedom came at no price

# Suddenly

plumes of smoke
flames surge in waves
tiny structures consumed in rage
clouds sit like aristocracy
waiting to emerge victorious
burning what was doesn't change what is
all that exists will remain to exist
just charred, or earth
cleanse
rebirth

# "Kiddy tea"

When the world wears your skin too thin
And the rough feels far too coarse
When words spoken to you are terse
And apologies shared show little remorse

When the train is running three hours late
And you miss an impressive meeting
When your friends forget an important date
And all your free moments feel fleeting

When you lose a piece you're been working on
And are the victim of a failed auto save
When you find out a deadline is too far gone
And your new phone soon meets it grave

When the simplest of tasks weigh a tonne
And your self care routine is down in flames
When you go to cook and the olive oils gone
And you succumb to disproportionate rage

I promise you no matter what befalls you today
You can spend a crap evening just with me
We don't have to over complicate
I can even make kiddy tea

# A piece of advice

If you join a "Zoom" call make sure you are on mute
If you fail to do this and should do a fart
You will end up on spotlight mode
Because it thinks you're talking
You're welcome